STAR FILES

Mary-Kate and Ashley Olsen

Stephanie Fitzgerald

Raintree

Chicago, Illinois

For more information address the publisher:
Raintree, 100 N. LaSalle, Suite 1200, Chicago IL 60602

Printed and bound in China by South China Printing Company

09 08 07 06
10 9 8 7 6 5 4 3 2 1

Library of Congress Cataloging-in-Publication Data:

Fitzgerald, Stephanie.
    Mary-Kate and Ashley Olsen / Stephanie Fitzgerald.
        p. cm. -- (Star Files)
    Includes bibliographical references and index.
    ISBN 1-4109-1662-6 (libray binding--hardcover)
    1. Olsen, Ashley, 1986---Juvenile literature. 2. Olsen, Mary-Kate, 1986--- Juvenile literature. 3. Actors--United States--Biography--Juvenile literature. I. Title. II. Series.
    PN2287.036F58 2005
    792.02'8'092273--dc22

                            2005005247

Acknowledgments
The publishers would like to thank the following for permission to reproduce photographs: Allstar Picture Library pp. **11**, **16**, **17** (l), **17** (r), **19**, **40** (t); Corbis pp. **9** (r) (Peter Freed), **10**, **13**, **25**, **34** (Fred Prouser/Reuters), **35** (r), **37**, **39** (t) (Lucy Nicholson/Reuters); Getty Images pp. **12** (t), **12** (b), **21** (t), **21** (b), **22** (t), **28** (Barbara Binstein), **42** (t) (Peter Kramer); Retna Pictures pp. **5** (Grayson Alexander), **6** (ABC/Photofest), **9** (l) (ABC/Photofest), **23** (Gregorio Binuya), **24** (Walter McBride), **26** (Walter McBride), **29** (Joseph Marzullo); Rex Features pp. **4** (Matt Baron), **7** (E Charbonneau/BEI), **8** (Peter Brooker), **14** (Peter Brooker), **15** (Peter Brooker), **18** (STK), **20** (THH), **22** (b) (Mirek Towski), **27** (t) (Stewart Cook), **27** (b) (Charles Sykes), **30** (TS/Keystone USA), **31** (t) (Action Press), **31** (b) (PF/Keystone USA), **32** (Anders Krusberg), **33** (Mirek Towski), **35** (l) (Peter Brooker), **36** (l) (Charles Sykes), **36** (r) (Mirek Towski), **38** (Sipa Press), **39** (b) (Peter Brooker), **40** (b), **41**, **42** (b) (Steve Connolly), **43**. Cover photograph reproduced with permission of Rex Features.

Quote sources: pp. **9**, **10**, **21** *Mary-Kate & Ashley: Our Story, updated edition: The Official Biography*, Mary-Kate & Ashley Olsen; p. **14** *People Magazine,* January 27, 2003; p. **25** *Entertainment Weekly*, May 21, 2004; p. **37** The Associated Press.

The publishers would like to thank Charly Rimsa for her assistance in the preparation of this book.

Contents

Any words appearing in the text in bold, **like this**, are explained in the glossary. You can also look out for them in the "Star Words" box at the bottom of each page.

Wonder Twins

Mary-Kate and Ashley Olsen are two of the most famous kids in the world. They started in show business when they were only 9 months old. Now the sisters are famous for their television shows, movies, videos, and even their clothing line. Now that they are grown up they attend the best movie **premieres**, fashion shows, and parties.

ALL ABOUT MARY-KATE AND ASHLEY

Full names: Ashley Fuller Olsen; Mary-Kate Olsen
Born: June 13, 1986 (Ashley is older by 2 minutes)
Place of birth: Sherman Oaks, California
Height: Ashley is 5 feet 3 inches (1 meter 57 centimeters); Mary-Kate is 5 feet 2 inches (1 meter 59 centimeters)
Hair: Blonde
Eyes: Blue-green
Family: Jarnette (mother), Dave (father), Trent (older brother), Lizzie (younger sister), McKenzie (stepmother), Taylor (half sister), Jake (half brother)

Star Words   executive manager in a business

A new hair color for Mary-Kate (right) makes it easier to tell the sisters apart.

Find out later

What was the first television show the twins appeared on?

Regular gals

Ashley and Mary-Kate are pretty and smart, and they make great movies. The thing that makes them so popular is that they are regular kids—just like you and your friends. They come from a large family that includes big brother Trent, little sister Lizzie, half brother Jake, and half sister Taylor.

Which actress is one of the girls' favorites?

Keeping it real

Mary-Kate and Ashley are very rich. They are each worth about $150 million. Even when they were little they made a lot of money. However, when they lived at home, they still had to do chores to earn their allowance. Ashley did the vacuuming. Mary-Kate fed the dogs. Both girls had to keep their rooms clean.

Once they turned eighteen in 2004, Ashley and Mary-Kate became co-presidents of their company, Dualstar. The sisters are the youngest executives in the world. They run a company that makes billions of dollars every year.

What was Mary-Kate and Ashley's first grown-up movie called?

premiere first showing of a movie, often with celebrities invited

Show business

In 1990, the girls' father realized that they would need business help. He hired a lawyer named Robert Thorne to be their manager. In 1993, when the sisters were 7 years old, they and Thorne created a company called Dualstar.

★ ★ ★ ★ ★ ★ ★ ★ ★

Twice as nice

Mary-Kate and Ashley were born in Sherman Oaks, California. This is a **suburb** of Los Angeles. The sisters are **fraternal twins**. Even though it is hard to tell them apart, they do not look exactly alike.

Their big break

When Mary-Kate and Ashley were 9 months old, their mom took them for their first and only **audition**. It was for a part on a sitcom called *Full House*. As soon as the show's **producer** saw Mary-Kate and Ashley, he knew he had found his stars. The producer had hired another set of twins for the part. However, he quickly replaced them with the Olsen sisters.

Star fact

At first, the producers of *Full House* did not want anyone to know that two girls played Michelle. They credited the part to Mary Kate Ashley Olsen.

The *Full House* cast included (from left) Jodi Sweetin, Bob Saget, Candace Cameron, John Stamos, and Dave Coulier.

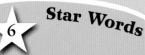
audition interview for an actor or musician, where they show their skills

Mary-Kate and Ashley are still close with their former *Full House* costars. They are pictured here in 2004 with their TV dad Bob Saget.

TV family

Mary-Kate and Ashley grew close to the actors who played their on-screen family. Candace Cameron and Jodi Sweetin played big sisters DJ and Stephanie. Bob Saget played the girls' dad. He had help from Uncle Jesse (John Stamos) and Joey (David Coulier).

Seeing double

Mary-Kate and Ashley shared the part of Michelle Tanner on *Full House* from 1987 through 1995. It is a law that children cannot work too many hours in a row. That is why twins often share a part on a television show or movie.

The girls quickly made Michelle Tanner one of the most popular characters on television. Even though it was their mom that got Mary-Kate and Ashley started in show business, the two do not feel they were ever pushed into acting. Ashley and Mary-Kate knew they could quit any time they wanted.

producer movie or television producers organize the people and money to make a movie or television show

John Stamos (above) first gained fame as Blackie Parish on ABC's popular soap opera, *General Hospital*. He was on the show from 1982 through 1984. Stamos is also a musician. He once played drums with the Beach Boys. You can see him in the Beach Boys' 1988 music video for "Kokomo."

Smile for the camera

Mary-Kate and Ashley were just babies when they started on *Full House*. They needed a lot of help from their acting coaches. These coaches are also called "baby wranglers." When the script called for Michelle to smile or giggle, an acting coach would hold a cookie off-stage.

★ Star fact

When they were young, the girls used to call their *Full House* costars by their character names. This helped keep them from messing up the taping of the show!

Sensitive or tough?

As the girls got a little older, they learned their lines by copying their coach. The coach would say the line, then Mary-Kate or Ashley would repeat it. Then the coach's voice would be cut from the show tape. Soon, the sisters' **distinct** personalities became clearer. The **directors** decided that they would use Ashley for **sensitive** scenes. Mary-Kate was called on to play Michelle when she had to be tough or funny.

Hard work pays off

Mary-Kate and Ashley spent 9 years on *Full House*. They grew up right before their fans' eyes! As they got older, they learned to memorize their scripts just like the other actors. Throughout the years, the sisters took acting lessons to improve their skills.

When *Full House* went off the air in 1995, it was sad for Mary-Kate and Ashley. They would miss their television family. They were ready for their next challenge, though.

> **"** We grew up around all the people on *Full House*, that's what made it so much fun for us to go to work every day. (Mary-Kate) **"**

Can you tell which Olsen sister is which?

Which one is which?

When the girls were babies, their parents used their freckles to tell them apart. Another difference between them is that Ashley is right-handed and Mary-Kate is left-handed.

Michelle jams with Uncle Jesse in this episode of *Full House*.

distinct different from someone else

Mary-Kate's horses

Mary-Kate fell in love for the first time on the set of *To Grandmother's House We Go*. It was with a pony named Four-by-Four. Now she has two horses, C.D. and Star. Mary-Kate has won trophies for competing in horse shows.

Take two!

Sharing a part on a sitcom was fun. By 1992, however, Mary-Kate and Ashley were ready for another challenge.

They starred in—and **produced**—their first television movie. It was called *To Grandmother's House We Go*.

> ❝ I'd go for a riding lesson every day if I could. (Mary-Kate) ❞

Big-time producers

The sisters had started their company, Dualstar, in 1990 to have more control over their **careers**. Now when they made a movie or television show they would also produce it. That meant the girls could make movies about the things they liked.

⭐ Star fact

By executive producing *To Grandmother's House We Go* at age six, Mary-Kate and Ashley became the youngest producers in history. An executive producer provides the money to make the movie. The producer has more creative control over the film.

Mary-Kate and Ashley in a scene from *To Grandmother's House We Go*.

Star Words   career what someone does for a job

Eugene Levy (shown here with costar Catherine O'Hara) starred in *Best in Show* and in the Olsens' 2004 movie, *New York Minute.*

They could choose what the movie was about, where it was filmed, and who their costars were. Nobody else—not even the **director**—had as much creative control.

Cover for me!

A week before filming began on *To Grandmother's House We Go*, Mary-Kate scratched her eye while she was playing. It was red for weeks. The director avoided filming Mary-Kate's red eye as much as possible. When it was time to film an important dinner scene between the two girls, it was too hard to hide the eye. Ashley had to dress like her sister and play both parts!

Favorite movies

Mary-Kate and Ashley liked musicals when they were little. Now they like comedies, too. Some of their favorite movies include:

Oklahoma! (1955)

West Side Story (1961)

My Fair Lady (1964)

Waiting for Guffman (1996)

Best in Show (2000)

More movies

The girls starred in several made-for-television movies over the next 2 years. *Double, Double, Toil and Trouble* was a Halloween movie. *How the West was Fun* was about the girls' adventures in the Old West. They also made several television specials, such as *The Olsen Twins' Mother's Day Special* and *How I Spent my Summer Vacation*.

Going to Hawaii

For *You're Invited to Mary-Kate & Ashley's Hawaiian Beach Party,* the whole family got to vacation in Hawaii (above). During the trip, the twins filmed a total of four different videos. They always worked hard!

Ashley and Mary-Kate took a magic carpet ride in their *Mother's Day Special*, which aired in 1993.

Star Words

direct-to-video movie made for video release, not for release in theaters

Private eyes

In 1994, when they were 8, Mary-Kate and Ashley made their first **direct-to-video** 30-minute movie. It was called *The Adventures of Mary-Kate & Ashley: The Case of Thorn Mansion*. In this film, the girls played detectives nicknamed "the Trenchcoat Twins." Their **motto** was "will solve any crime by dinner time." Over the next 6 years, they made 11 Trenchcoat Twins films.

Join the party

Mary-Kate and Ashley's next series of videos was based on their real lives. Both girls love to spend time with their friends and have fun. They took their own likes and set them to music. A fun new series was born. *You're Invited to Mary-Kate & Ashley's . . .* was a series of ten party videos hosted by the sisters. The titles included a sleepover party, a Hawaiian beach party, and a ballet party.

Just like me

Mary-Kate and Ashley are involved in every part of their movies. They try to put a little bit of themselves into everything they do. For example, Ashley loves ballet. That is where the idea for *You're Invited to Mary-Kate & Ashley's Ballet Party* came from.

Ashley and her mom Jarnette are both good ballet dancers.

Ashley at the ballet

Ballet Party featured the famous New York City Ballet. In the movie, Ashley got to live her dream. She got the chance to share the stage with dancers from the world-famous Juilliard School in New York City.

A Family Affair

Lizzie Olsen

Little sister Lizzie has appeared in several *The Adventures of Mary-Kate and Ashley* videos. She also acts in plays at local theaters. Even though Lizzie enjoys acting, she has not made it her job . . . yet.

★ Star fact

The twins' manager, Robert Thorne, praises their family for keeping them normal. He says the girls' parents "raised them not to be impressed with themselves. They live really normal lives."

In 1996 Ashley and Mary-Kate were enjoying a lot of success with their videos. All of the kids who loved Michelle Tanner wanted to see everything Mary-Kate and Ashley appeared in. However, things at home were not going so well.

Break up

Just a year after the sisters lost their television family, their real-life family went through a split. When Mary-Kate and Ashley were 9 years old, their parents got divorced. Luckily the girls had a loving family—and each other—to help them through this difficult time.

Twice the fun

After the divorce, Mary-Kate and Ashley split their time between their mom's house and their dad's. They both had their own rooms—and plenty of pets— at both places.

The girls' mom Jarnette gave them their start in acting.

Star Words pitfalls problems or dangers

After the girls' father married stepmother McKenzie, Ashley and Mary-Kate's family got even bigger. In addition to older brother Trent and little sister Lizzie, the girls have another younger half sister named Taylor and a half brother named Jake.

Real life

Ashley and Mary-Kate give their family a lot of credit for keeping them "normal." Their dad says that with six kids in the house, he had to be strict! Mary-Kate and Ashley never got special privileges just because they were famous. This helped them avoid the **pitfalls** that other child stars often fall into, such as drinking alcohol.

Mary-Kate and Ashley's family in 2004: (from left) Dave, Jake, McKenzie, Mary-Kate, Taylor, Ashley, Lizzie, and Trent.

Lights, Camera, Action!

The Parent Trap

The story of *It Takes Two* is similar to the movie *The Parent Trap*. This was first made in 1961. It was remade in 1998 with Lindsay Lohan. In the film, Lohan plays twins who were separated as babies. When the girls meet up later in life, they try to get their divorced parents back together.

When *Full House* ended in 1995, Mary-Kate and Ashley made the move to the big screen. They starred in their first **feature film** called *It Takes Two*. The girls played identical-looking strangers called Alyssa and Amanda. They plot to get Alyssa's father to fall in love with Amanda's **guardian.**

A whole new ball game

Shooting a full-length feature film is very different than being on a television show or in a 30-minute video. Movies are usually 90 minutes to 2 hours long. Mary-Kate and Ashley had to memorize a lot more lines than ever before. Shooting the movie took longer than anything they had worked on up until now.

For 1998's *The Parent Trap*, Lindsay Lohan had a dual part playing twins.

Star Words   feature film movie that is shown in theaters

Extra responsibilities

The girls were also **producers** of this movie. They had to think about all the different sets they would need. They had to help choose a whole cast of actors. They even had to help decide what type of songs would go on the **soundtrack**. It is unusual for stars to take that active a part in producing a movie. It is even more unusual for 9-year-old kids. No other actors in history have reached this level of control in show business at such a young age.

Smash hit

As usual, Mary-Kate and Ashley's hard work paid off. *It Takes Two* earned more than $19 million. The girls were true movie stars!

Famous costars

Mary-Kate and Ashley had two famous costars in *It Takes Two*. They were Kirstie Alley and Steve Guttenberg (above). Alley is best known for playing Rebecca on the sitcom *Cheers*. Guttenberg has been in films such as *Three Men and a Baby, Cocoon,* and *Police Academy*.

For *It Takes Two*, Mary-Kate played a streetwise orphan named Amanda. Ashley played her rich look-alike, Alyssa.

guardian someone who is not your real parent, but who is responsible for looking after you

Caught on tape

The girls made their first feature-length **direct-to-video** movie in 1998. The film was called *Billboard Dad*. Mary-Kate and Ashley played sisters who were trying to find a wife for their father.

The girls went on to make 8 more 90-minute videos, including *Passport to Paris*. They made that movie in 1999, when they were 13 years old. On that film, the girls each had their first ever on-screen kiss—in front of the whole cast and crew! From the way Mary-Kate acted, the **director** thought it was probably her first kiss ever.

First on screen

The girls actually had their first big screen moment in 1994. It was a brief one. They are part of a slumber party scene in the movie version of *The Little Rascals.*

Mary-Kate and Ashley were joined by their real-life dad for the **premiere** of *Billboard Dad.*

Charlie's Angels: Full Throttle starred (from left) Drew Barrymore, Cameron Diaz, and Lucy Liu.

Star fact

The Olsen sisters have made more than 30 direct-to-video movies. The videos have sold more than 17 million copies worldwide.

Movie magic

In *Getting There*, a 90-minute video made in 2002, the girls were supposed to be driving to Utah. However, they only had learners' permits. They were not allowed to drive without an adult in the car! Instead of having the girls drive, the director had the car towed along the road.

Oops!

There are always on-set problems that have to be worked around. When the girls were filming *The Challenge* in Mexico they faced a real-life challenge. The crew was not used to the food and water there, and everyone got sick! One of the actresses on *Getting There* broke her leg during filming. The script had to be reworked at the last minute to explain the actress' leg cast!

Charlie's Angels

Actress Drew Barrymore called Mary-Kate and Ashley personally to ask them to appear in her 2003 movie *Charlie's Angels: Full Throttle*. The sisters play future angels in the movie.

19

Fake teeth

Mary-Kate and Ashley were 9 years old when they made *The Case of the U.S. Space Camp Mission*. They were losing their baby teeth and had to wear fake ones, called flippers, during filming.

Location, location, location

When Mary-Kate and Ashley make a movie, they often pick a fun city to visit. They can decide where to go, because they are the **producers** of their movies. Being in movies has allowed them to spend time in Paris, Rome, London, and Hawaii.

To the moon

One of the most exciting locations Ashley and Mary-Kate have been to is Huntsville, Alabama. In 1996, they filmed at a U.S. space camp there. The movie they were shooting was called *The Adventures of Mary-Kate & Ashley: The Case of the U.S. Space Camp Mission*.

1996 was another busy year for Mary-Kate and Ashley.

Star Words honored special

The sisters, their older brother Trent, and their dad Dave all got to spend a week at space camp. They were given jobs to carry out on a pretend space shuttle mission. The girls dressed in astronaut suits for the movie. They even got to ride in a space simulator, where they felt what it is like to walk on the Moon.

Dinner for three

One of the best parts of the sisters' trip was having dinner with Alan Bean. He was the fourth U.S. astronaut to walk on the moon during the *Apollo 12* mission in 1969. "We felt so **honored** to have dinner with one of only twelve people on Earth who have ever touched the Moon," Ashley said.

Favorite cities

Mary-Kate's favorite city is Rome. She says she loves the culture and history of Italy. Ashley prefers the romance of Paris (above). Both girls also adore the bright lights and energy of New York City.

The girls were excited to meet astronaut Alan Bean.

21

School days

Mary-Kate and Ashley were so busy—where did they find time for school? People think child actors do not have to go to school. They have to take their lessons, though! It is just that their schooling is organized a little differently.

Ashley and Mary-Kate rarely had the chance to take classes in a regular classroom when they were little.

Set for class

When Mary-Kate and Ashley were not on the set of a movie or television show, they went to school like everyone else. When the sisters were filming a television show, they were working at the same place every day. This meant that they could have a classroom right at the **studio.** This class looked just like any other, with desks, computers, and a chalkboard.

Studies

Mary-Kate and Ashley were very serious about their studies. They say they have their parents to thank for that. The sisters always knew that they wanted to go to college. They also knew that they would have to work hard to get there.

It's a wonder Mary-Kate and Ashley ever had time for school! Here they are at the **premiere** of the movie *Alaska* in 1996.

Star Words   competitive trying to do better than others

Mary-Kate and Ashley are very close. A little friendly competition helped them both do better in school.

No free rides

Mary-Kate and Ashley's studio teachers gave the girls all the same tests and homework they would get at a regular school. There were usually two teachers. One taught language arts, French, and social studies. The other taught math and science.

★ Star fact

Ashley's favorite subject in school was math. Mary-Kate's favorite subject was English.

Competition

Mary-Kate and Ashley were very **competitive** about their school grades. They did not get mad at each other, though. If one sister did better in a subject, it pushed the other to work harder.

Crazy classrooms

When the girls were on location filming a movie, class was held wherever they could find a space. Sometimes the classroom was set up in a trailer, which was the girls' private space during filming. Other times, Mary-Kate and Ashley had classes in a hotel lobby.

studio building where shows or movies are filmed

Hitting the Books

The books
Mary-Kate and Ashley's book series include:

The Adventures of Mary-Kate & Ashley

The New Adventures of Mary-Kate & Ashley

Mary-Kate & Ashley's Sweet 16 Series

Mary-Kate & Ashley Starring In...

Mary-Kate & Ashley in ACTION

Graduation Summer

Mary-Kate and Ashley are always looking for new things to try. They decided to release a series of books based on their *The Adventures of Mary-Kate & Ashley* videos. There was a book for every episode of the mystery series.

The books were very popular. Then, in 1998, the Olsens launched a new book series called *The New Adventures of Mary-Kate & Ashley*. These books were not based on the videos. They featured all new mysteries for the Trenchcoat Twins to solve.

Even when they were only twelve, the Olsen sisters were very successful.

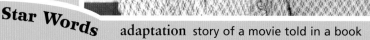

Sister stories

Many more book series followed *The Adventures . . .* and *New Adventures . . .* series. As with all of their projects, the sisters had a lot of input into these books. Mary-Kate and Ashley would talk to **editors** about the kind of stories they wanted to tell.

They wanted to make sure the books reflected their own personalities. Some of the books were based on the characters in their television series. Others were **adaptations** of their movies.

Star fact

A lot of people wonder why the Olsen sisters are so successful. Susan Schulz, Editor in Chief of the magazine *CosmoGIRL!*, has an idea. "They are very popular because teenagers have grown up with them ... they're real," she says.

Book lover

Mary-Kate is serious about books. Her favorite subjects in high school were English and creative writing. That also helps when she and Ashley are looking over the scripts for their movies and shows.

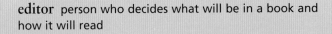

Mary-Kate enjoys reading and creative writing.

editor person who decides what will be in a book and how it will read

25

Cue the Music

★ ★ ★ ★ ★ ★ ★ ★ ★

The music

Mary-Kate and Ashley have performed on more than ten CDs, including: *Brother for Sale, I Am The Cute One, Cool Yule, You're Invited to Mary-Kate and Ashley's Birthday Party, You're Invited to Mary-Kate and Ashley's Ballet Party, You're Invited to Mary-Kate and Ashley's Sleepover Party, The Adventures of Mary-Kate & Ashley Give Us A Mystery, Greatest Hits I, Greatest Hits II,* and *Greatest Hits III.*

★ ★ ★ ★ ★ ★ ★ ★ ★

Mary-Kate and Ashley have always been busy with their acting and books. Then they managed to find time to record music.

Oh brother!

The girls' first CD, which they recorded in 1992, was called *Brother for Sale.* You can bet big brother Trent was not too happy about that! Mary-Kate liked to tease him by saying that the title song was her favorite.

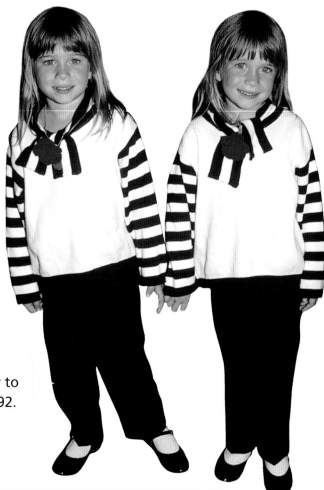

Ashley and Mary-Kate look like they are ready to become pop stars in 1992.

Star Words

choreographer person who makes up dance steps and teaches them to others.

Mary-Kate and Ashley play an active part in choosing the music for their movies.

A first for everything

The sisters' CDs were so popular that they decided to make music videos to go along. Their first one was called *Our First Video*. It featured songs from their first two CDs, *Brother for Sale* and *I Am the Cute One*.

The girls had a **choreographer** to teach them dance moves. However, the video is mostly just the two of them having a good time, jumping around on a bed. After all, they were only 7 years old at the time!

A new tune

In recent years, Mary-Kate and Ashley have continued to be involved in music. They have not made their own music, however. The girls are very involved in picking the music for their movies. Now Dualstar also releases CDs of the Olsens' movie **soundtracks**.

Star fact

To celebrate the success of *Our First Video*, the girls took eight of their friends out for hamburgers and milkshakes. They even rode in a limousine!

The joker

Mary-Kate (below) is a bit of a joker. She likes to play tricks on her friends. She once tricked her dad into thinking she had gotten a tattoo. It was really just a temporary **henna** tattoo, though.

henna reddish dye that is made from leaves

Back to the Small Screen

Riley and Chloe

The girls played Riley and Chloe Carlson in their video *Winning London* and in *So Little Time*. In the film, Mary-Kate played Chloe and Ashley played Riley. On *So Little Time*, they switched names.

In 1998, when they were 12 years old, Mary-Kate and Ashley decided to return to television. That year, they starred in their first series since *Full House*.

It Takes TWO

In ABC's *TWO of a Kind*, the girls played twin sisters who lived with their single dad in Chicago. The show lasted only one season.

One more time

In 2001, when they were fifteen, the girls launched a new television series called *So Little Time*. Although they enjoyed working on the series, they stopped after one season. They had an agreement with Warner Brothers studios to make a movie before they went away to college. If they continued on television, there would be no time to make the movie. *So Little Time* was turned into a book series in 2002.

In 2001, Mary-Kate and Ashley were busy making the television series *So Little Time*.

Star Words

nominated put forward as one of the right people to win an award

Ashley and Mary-Kate attended the 2001 Emmy awards together—of course!

Awards

In 2001, Mary-Kate was **nominated** for a daytime Emmy award for her role on *So Little Time.* She did not win. However, just 2 years earlier, both sisters won the Favorite Television Actresses award at the Nickelodeon Kid's Choice Awards.

Action!

That same year, the girls **produced** and starred in an animated show for Nickelodeon. The show was called *Mary-Kate and Ashley in ACTION!* For this series, the sisters lent their voices to the characters of Special Agent Misty and Special Agent Amber. Misty and Amber travel the world fighting crime. The girls created a book series to go with this show as well.

 **Star fact**

Mary-Kate does not think that she and her sister look alike at all!

29

Branded

Mary-Kate and Ashley have placed their names on a lot of different products. This is called creating a brand identity, or **branding**. It means that the girls are linked with the products. Often the people who buy the products want to be just like the girls.

Fashion forward

In 2001, Mary-Kate and Ashley developed their own fashion line for Wal-Mart. They did this with the help of designer Judy Swartz. Judy created the girls' **wardrobe** for *TWO of a Kind*. They were 12 years old when they made that series. Judy took adult outfits and **tailored** them to fit Mary-Kate and Ashley. Fans of the show loved the girls' clothes. They wanted to buy the same styles. That is when Mary-Kate and Ashley decided to start their own line of fashion.

Turned down

Mary-Kate and Ashley are very picky about what they give their names to. Some products they have turned down include canned spaghetti, fruit snacks, and wrapping paper.

Getting their clothing line off the ground was a lot of work for Ashley and Mary-Kate.

Star Words

tailor change the size of a piece of clothing to fit the wearer perfectly

Mary-Kate and Ashley announce plans for their very successful brand.

Accessories

The Olsen sisters both love accessories, such as handbags, bracelets, necklaces, and shoes. Mary-Kate says she can never have enough watches. Ashley has a large collection of shoes. Both girls love to wear flip-flops.

Tailor made

Mary-Kate and Ashley are very involved in creating the fashions for the mary-kateandashley line. Sometimes the clothes are based on outfits from the girls' movies. Often, Judy will suggest a look or style. In either case, the girls only approve styles that they like and that they would wear themselves.

★ Star fact

In 2003, the mary-kate andashley line earned $1 billion in sales.

Something extra

Mary-kateandashley clothes quickly became the most popular teen and "tween" fashions on the market. Before long, Mary-Kate and Ashley expanded the line to include cosmetics, accessories, fragrances, sheets, comforters, and even toothpaste! By 2003, mary-kateandashley products were being sold around the world.

tween ages in between little kids and teenagers
wardrobe clothes worn for a show, play, or movie

Living dolls

Mary-Kate and Ashley have a line of fashion dolls. They created these dolls with Mattel. That is the same toy company that makes Barbie dolls. The first group of Mary-Kate and Ashley dolls came out in 2000. These dolls have short hair and look like the sisters did when they starred on *TWO of a Kind*.

In 2002, Mattel brought out the new Mary-Kate and Ashley Sweet 16 dolls. That was the year the sisters really turned sixteen. These dolls look more grown-up than the first line of Mary-Kate and Ashley dolls. They wear more grown-up clothes and have longer hair, like the girls did at the time.

Birthday party

The girls had a surprise birthday party when they were sixteen. The party was held at their favorite restaurant. The girls had a cake decorated with a California license plate.

Mary-Kate and Ashley show off their first fashion dolls in 2000.

Star Words   theme topic or subject

These sweet sixteen-year-olds look ready to hit the road!

New cars

When Mary-Kate and Ashley turned sixteen, they were both given brand new cars! Mary-Kate received a green Range Rover. Ashley's is black. Driving their new cars quickly became one of the girls' favorite hobbies!

Game time

A lot of games for Playstation and GameBoy systems are geared toward boys. Ashley and Mary-Kate wanted to make games that girls would like. So they released their own line of video games.

Again, they chose **themes** that reflected what was going on in their lives. *Winners Circle* features Mary-Kate and Ashley on horseback. In *Sweet-16 Licensed to Drive*, players are invited to a birthday celebration. Players get to take a driver's test, surf, and go rock climbing. These are all things that Mary-Kate and Ashley love to do.

Facing Trouble

Anorexia

Anorexia nervosa is an eating disorder. This is a complicated disease because there are a lot of emotional issues tied to it. People suffering from anorexia often think they are fat even if they are really thin. They stop eating in order to avoid gaining weight.

It is very hard to keep your privacy when you have grown up in the spotlight. The **media** watches every move the Olsen sisters make. Then they report it to the world. Some people even make up bad stories about the girls just to sell magazines.

Bump in the road

In 2004 Mary-Kate entered a **rehabilitation center** to deal with her eating disorder. Because she was so thin, some reporters said that Mary-Kate had a drug problem. That was not true. According to her dad, Mary-Kate had been struggling with **anorexia** for 2 years.

Although the girls love their fans, it is sometimes hard to be in the public eye all the time.

Star Words

anorexia eating disorder

> Anorexia can happen to anyone—even someone as beautiful and successful as Mary-Kate.

Being in the media

The term "media" includes everything from television news to magazines to newspapers. Throughout their **careers**, the Olsen sisters have been featured in more than 100,000 newspaper stories!

Getting better

Mary-Kate had already gained about 10 pounds (4.5 kilograms) just 10 days after her release from rehab in July 2004. She attends group therapy every week and is working with a **nutritionist.** Hopefully Mary-Kate is well on the road to recovery.

A lot of people are watching Mary-Kate closely. Magazines and television shows report on every move she makes. They take pictures to show how thin she is. A representative for the Olsens reminds Mary-Kate's fans that a cure cannot happen overnight. It will take a while for Mary-Kate to be completely well, but that does not mean that she is not getting better.

media types of communication such as television, radio, newspapers, and magazines

Julia Roberts has starred in many movies, including *Pretty Woman, Erin Brockovich, Notting Hill,* and *My Best Friend's Wedding.*

Two for one

It is funny to think about Mary-Kate and Ashley as real people. Because they grew up on television, a lot of people feel like they really know the girls. Of course, the characters Mary-Kate and Ashley have played over the years are not real.

Favorite actors

Some of Mary-Kate and Ashley's favorite actors include:

Cameron Diaz

Drew Barrymore

Julia Roberts

Following their individual fashion sense helps keep the sisters looking unique.

Star Words   unique different from everyone else

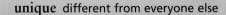

Without doubt, the sisters have a lot in common. However, it is important to remember that they are individuals. For many years, the girls were known simply as "the Olsen twins." That bothers them because they are both **unique** individuals. They each have their own personalities, likes, and dislikes.

Telling the difference

Both girls try to have healthy diets. They like to eat fish, fruits, and vegetables. They also like to stay in shape with kickboxing, yoga, and Pilates. In her free time, Mary-Kate also likes photography, drawing, and cooking. Ashley has her own interests, including dancing and playing tennis.

> It's nice when somebody calls me by name and doesn't say, 'Hey, you're an Olsen twin.'
> (Ashley)

Both sisters admit that Ashley is the worrier of the two. Mary-Kate has always been a little more easy-going. Mary-Kate likes to get up early, while Ashley likes to sleep in.

Yoga is a great form of exercise.

Keeping fit

Yoga (below) and Pilates are exercise routines that focus on the body and the mind. They use movements to make muscles stronger and to make the body more flexible. People who practice yoga and Pilates find it very relaxing.

Separation

Before Mary-Kate went away to get treatment for her eating disorder, the girls had only been separated once in their lives. That was for two weeks when they went away to camp.

Best friends forever

One thing you can be sure of: Ashley and Mary-Kate are the best of friends. Sure they fight sometimes—all sisters do! They know they can always count on each other, though. Each thinks the other is the smartest, prettiest, most fun person she knows. Of course Mary-Kate and Ashley each have a lot of their own friends. The girls do not share everything.

Getting personal

As the girls have gotten older, a lot of people have focused on their romantic lives. When you are a celebrity and your picture is always in the paper, a lot of **rumors** can get started. Any time Mary-Kate or Ashley is seen with a certain boy, it is reported that they are dating.

Ashley and Mary-Kate have always been very close.

Star Words

rumor story that a lot of people discuss, but that may not be true

> Mary-Kate and David Katzenberg are still good friends.

★ ★ ★ ★ ★ ★ ★ ★ ★

Hollywood stars

In 2004 Mary-Kate and Ashley were awarded a star on the Hollywood Walk of Fame (below). This is the most famous sidewalk in the world. Some of the biggest celebrities in the world have a star here with their name on it.

Young love

Both girls had boyfriends before they went away to college. Ashley was dating Matt Kaplan. He is a football player from Columbia University. Mary-Kate was dating David Katzenberg. His dad is Jeffrey Katzenberg, co-founder of Dreamworks SKG. That is a company that makes films, including *Shrek*, *Shark Tale*, and *Gladiator*.

Moving on

Once Mary-Kate and Ashley went away to college, it was hard to keep up their old relationships. More recently, Ashley was linked to Scott Sartiano, who lives in New York City. Ashley and Scott seemed to enjoy each other's company. Mary-Kate was said to be dating Scott's friend Ali Fatourechi.

Back to the big screen

The year 2004 was very exciting for Ashley and Mary-Kate. In May they released *New York Minute*. This was their first big screen feature in almost 10 years. The difference now was that Mary-Kate and Ashley were grown up. This was a more mature movie that the girls hoped would appeal to an older audience. As with all of their movies, television shows, and videos, Ashley and Mary-Kate **produced** *New York Minute*.

Mary-Kate and Ashley on the set of *New York Minute.*

Eugene Levy

For *New York Minute*, the girls wanted to costar with Eugene Levy (above). He is a very popular comedy actor. He has also starred in two of the girls' favorite films, *Best in Show* and *Waiting for Guffman.*

Who's the boss?

As executive producers, Mary-Kate and Ashley own their movies and shows. They also have a lot of say about how a movie or show is made. They help come up with the stories. They approve the scripts. They even help pick the other actors in the story. All of this—plus acting—is a lot of work. Especially for two kids! Mary-Kate and Ashley manage to make it work. After all, they have been in show business their entire lives.

Big business

More than 60 people work at the Dualstar offices in California. The offices are full of shelves packed with Mary-Kate and Ashley's products. Dualstar oversees all of the Olsen's movies, television shows, books, music, and licensed products, such as clothes, toys, and beauty products.

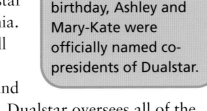

★ Star fact

On their eighteenth birthday, Ashley and Mary-Kate were officially named co-presidents of Dualstar.

Soundtracks

Ashley and Mary-Kate pick the music for their movies' **soundtracks**. For *New York Minute,* the girls asked the band Simple Plan to play on the soundtrack and to appear in the film.

Ashley and Mary-Kate pose with the guys from Simple Plan.

41

What's next

In the fall of 2004, Ashley and Mary-Kate started classes at New York University. The sisters have bodyguards while they are away at school. However, they try to blend in with the other students as much as possible. They think of themselves as regular teenagers. They want everyone else to see them that way, too.

Home away from home

Of course, not many college freshmen have the type of living arrangements the Olsens do. They have a huge $7.3 million **penthouse** apartment near school. It has four bedrooms, a screening room, and a study for each sister.

The sisters live in this luxury apartment building while they go to school in New York.

★ ★ ★ ★ ★ ★ ★ ★

Eating out

Some of Mary-Kate and Ashley's favorite places to eat in New York include:

- Bread Tribeca, an Italian restaurant
- Pastis, a popular restaurant in the meat-packing district
- Magnolia Bakery, for when they want something sweet
- Nobu, where they love to eat sushi.

★ ★ ★ ★ ★ ★ ★ ★

Mary-Kate will continue to attend therapy sessions and work with her **nutritionist**. Luckily, her class schedule is light. She can go home and visit with friends and family any time she needs to.

Ashley looks like any other student as she leaves class.

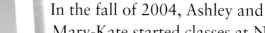

Star Words penthouse apartment on the top floor of a building

Duty calls

Of course, Ashley and Mary-Kate will also find time to squeeze work in among their studies. Dualstar had an office built near the girls' apartment so they can go to work in between classes.

Right now the girls are focusing on their studies. However, they are also thinking about the future. Both are interested in **directing** movies. Though they will probably continue to do movies together, they also plan to act separately. Maybe one of them will even direct the other in a film!

Dennie Gordon, shown here with the Olsens, directed *New York Minute*.

Directors

The director of a movie sets the overall tone of the film. She helps the actors understand what makes their characters tick. The director also gives the actors specific instructions on how to perform their parts.

Find Out More

Books

Britton, Tamara L. *Young Profiles: Mary-Kate & Ashley Olsen*. Edina, MN: Checkerboard Books, 2000.

Dougherty, Terri. *People in the News: The Olsen Twins*. San Diego, CA: Lucent Books, 2005.

Olsen, Mary-Kate & Ashley. *Mary-Kate & Ashley: Our Story*, Updated edition: The Official Biography. New York, NY: HarperEntertainment, 2003.

Russell, Bailey J. *Young Profiles: Mary-Kate & Ashley Olsen*. Edina, MN: Checkerboard Books, 2003

Tracy, Kathleen. *Blue Banner Biography: Mary-Kate and Ashley Olsen*. Bear, Delaware: Mitchell Lane Publishers, 2003.

Filmography

New York Minute (2004)
Charlie's Angels: Full Throttle (2003)
The Challenge (2003)
When In Rome (2002)
Getting There (2002)
Holiday in the Sun (2001)
Winning London (2001)
The Amazing Adventures of Mary-Kate & Ashley (2000)
Our Lips Are Sealed (2000)
You're Invited to... (ten movies made between 1997 and 2000)
Switching Goals (1999)

Passport to Paris (1999)
Billboard Dad (1998)
The Adventures of Mary-Kate & Ashley (ten
    movies made between 1994 and 1997)
It Takes Two (1995)
How the West Was Fun (1994)
The Little Rascals (1994)
Double, Double, Toil and Trouble (1993)
To Grandmother's House We Go (1992)

Television
Mary-Kate and Ashley in ACTION! (2001)
So Little Time (2001)
TWO of a Kind (1998)
Full House (1987–1995)

Glossary

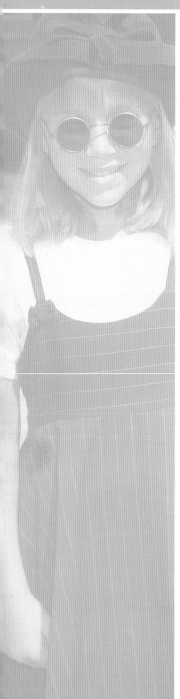

adaptation story of a movie told in a book

anorexia eating disorder

audition interview for an actor or musician, where they show their skills

branding when famous people get money for putting their name on a product. They hope the product will appeal to their fans.

career what someone does for a job

choreographer person who makes up dance steps and teaches them to others

competitive trying to do better than others

direct-to-video movie made for video release, not for release in theaters

director person in charge of making a movie or television show

distinct different from someone else

editor person who decides what will be in a book and how it will read

executive manager in a business

feature film movie that is shown in theaters

fraternal twins fraternal twins are born from two separate eggs that both grow inside the womb at the same time; identical twins are born from a single egg that splits in two

guardian someone who is not your real parent, but who is responsible for looking after you

henna reddish dye that is made from leaves

honored special

media types of communication such as television, radio, newspapers, and magazines

motto slogan or saying

nominated put forward as one of the right people to win an award

nutritionist person who can help others make smart, healthy food choices

penthouse apartment on the top floor of a building

pitfalls problems or dangers

premiere first showing of a movie, often with celebrities invited

producer movie or television producers organize the people and money to make a movie or television show

rehabilitation center treatment center where people go to recover from an illness such as an eating disorder

rumor story that a lot of people discuss, but that may not be true

sensitive emotional

soundtrack music used in a movie

studio building where shows or movies are filmed

suburb outskirts of a town or city where people live

tailor change the size of a piece of clothing to fit the wearer perfectly

theme topic or subject

tween ages in between little kids and teenagers

unique different from everyone else

wardrobe clothes worn for a show, play, or movie

Index